THE COMPLETE GUIDE TO NATURAL AND PERMANENT WEIGHT LOSS

M.P. Unwin

MINERVA PRESS

LONDON

MONTREUX LOS ANGELES SYDNEY

First Published 1997 by
MINERVA PRESS
195 Knightsbridge
London SW7 1RE

Printed in Great Britain for Minerva Press

THE COMPLETE GUIDE TO NATURAL AND PERMANENT WEIGHT LOSS

If you want to, you can.
If you persist, you will.
If you waver, you probably won't.
If you don't, you never will.

Introduction

Being overweight is not uncommon, one in five men and one in three women in Britain are in fact overweight. The question we must ask ourselves is why? The simple answer is that people do not know how to lose weight in the correct manner.

After reading the enclosed information, you will look at losing weight in a totally different way.

We have all seen the expensive advertising campaigns on the television and in newspapers and magazines, selling their unique pills and potions that are said to lose you pounds in a matter of days, guaranteed. Do they work? I am sure some people have had what they class as a benefit from these products, I cannot really comment, because I personally have not tried all of them. If I had decided to try them all I would be popping pills until I was seventy and working half a dozen jobs just to pay for them.

It is not just losing the weight that's the problem, it's keeping it off once you have lost it. How many times have you gone on a super strict diet eating no more that a celery stick and a bowl of muesli every day only to put the weight back on and more, once the diet has finished? Sound familiar? Don't panic, you are not on your own.

Then of course there are the weight classes, where you go and spend good money to let someone weigh and measure you, a job you can certainly do for yourself. Don't get me wrong, these classes can be useful as a way of motivating yourself. After all, who wants to go to a class and be weighed in front of a crowd of people only to find you have not lost the weight you wanted, if any at all. As I have said, classes can be useful, but they are definitely not necessary in order for you to lose weight.

In short, if you read the enclosed information and keep referring to it in the future, I am confident that you will find it very useful in your battle to lose weight permanently.

Health Risks

I do not want to over emphasise the fact that being overweight is bad for you, but I feel that the subject must be raised.

You may be overweight due to genetic or hormonal reasons, in which case dieting may not prove effective, but it is true that the majority of overweight people are overweight simply because they consume too much food.

People who are over their ideal weight are more at risk from high blood pressure, raised blood fats, gout and diabetes. All of these factors increase the risk of heart attacks. Heart disease has become a great killer in these modern times, with some 180,000 deaths a year in Britain alone. The problem is that people always think that it is going to happen to someone else, but maybe the following figures will give you something to think about.

If you are overweight by 25% your life expectancy is reduced by 3.6 years.

If you are overweight by 35% your life expectancy is reduced by 4.3 years.

If you are overweight by 45% your life expectancy is reduced by 6.6 years.

If you are overweight by 55% your life expectancy is reduced by 11.4 years.

4 out of every 10 people who die prematurely, do so from some sort of heart condition.

I don't know about you, but I cannot see the point of eating yourself into an early grave.

Where Does It All Start?

Being overweight often begins at childhood, overweight parents tend to have overweight children, and these children tend to grow into overweight adults themselves, who tend to have overweight children, and so the circle continues.

In comparison, normal weight parents tend to have normal weight children.

If both parents are of normal weight, approximately 10% of children are overweight.

If one parent is overweight, approximately 40% of children are overweight.

If both parents are overweight, approximately 80% of children are overweight.

80% of overweight children grow into overweight adults.

Although being overweight may be a problem inherited from parents, it is much more likely that their children have simply learned their parents' bad eating habits.

The Guilt Trip

I am fat and ugly, nobody likes me, or wants me. I might as well stay fat.

I am lazy, I have no will power and it is my fault that I cannot lose weight.

I am worth nothing, I am fat because I am not a very nice person, therefore I deserve to be fat.

I don't like being fat, it depresses me. I am depressed, so I will cheer myself up by eating.

Give yourself a day off and stop feeling sorry for yourself, it will change nothing. This may be harsh, but you do have to put things into perspective. If you want to lose weight you can, but nobody else can do it for you.

Why Do You Want to Lose Weight?

Having previously read about the health risks involved in being overweight, surprisingly this is not the main reason for most people wanting to lose weight. The main reason is society, today a lot of people think that they have got to lose weight in order to meet with society's ideals. After all, slim people are more attractive to the opposite sex, they are more intelligent, they have more self control, they are more successful and are generally much happier and nicer people.

This is of course rubbish, but the truth is, society does discriminate against overweight people. How many of you have been stared at or whispered about just because you are larger than other people think you should be?

Let us forget about society for a moment, what about family. How many of you have been put under pressure into going on a diet, because your family or partner thinks you should? There is only one way that you will lose, and control your weight successfully and permanently, and that is because *you* want to. Unless *you* want to lose weight for yourself, forget it.

Unfair, But True

An overweight body has more of a tendency to store fat. Despite how much food it is consuming, it is nutritionally starved, which is due to continuously over-eating. Digestive juices are being overproduced, because the digestive system has been overloaded. This leads to a lack of important enzymes which are needed to provide nutrients to cells. Therefore, however much food the body consumes, it continues to crave for more.

Fat cells are a lot less active than the other cells found in the body. This means that fat cells do not burn as much energy as muscle cells, therefore an overweight person naturally has a slower metabolic rate, and in turn burns off fewer calories per pound, than a person of ideal weight. Simplified, an overweight person can consume very few calories and still have trouble losing weight.

This does not mean that if you are very overweight, there is no point in trying. It just means that it will take you longer to lose the same amount of weight, as it would for someone who is already slimmer than you.

Junk food, or food of no nutritional value encourages your body to eat. Because it is being starved of important vitamins, minerals and other essential nutrients that it requires, the body continues to crave for more and more calories in order to satisfy its needs.

Metabolic Rate

Your metabolic rate is the amount of energy/calories that is required to keep your body alive, when your body is at rest. Energy/calories are used to keep the heart, lungs and digestive system moving, to maintain the nerve impulse to and from the brain and for all the necessary chemical reactions to take place in the body.

Calories and Calorie Intake

A kilocalorie (Kcal) or calorie as it is commonly known, is a measurement of energy. The three main nutrients, fat, carbohydrate and protein, can all supply the body with energy.

1 gram of pure protein contains 4 calories.

1 gram of pure carbohydrate contains 3.75 calories.

1 gram of pure fat contains 9 calories.

The amount of calories the body needs, varies from person to person, depending on sex, height, build and the amount of exercise it does per day. Here are the approximate calories that are needed by the body per day.

	Female	Male
Teenager	2200	3000
Young adult	2100	3000
Middle-aged adult	2000	2500
Old-aged adult	1800	2300

You will find tables like this in many books and leaflets, in fact this table is out of one such publication. The trouble with such tables, is that they are as stated, approximate. This information is not good enough, you need to have a closer idea of what calories *your* body requires, based on *your* height, weight, sex and age. This is not difficult to work out for yourself, all you need is a pen, paper and perhaps a calculator.

Men	Women
Begin with a base of 66	Begin with a base of 65.5
Multiply your weight by 6.3 (in pounds)	Multiply your weight by 4.3 (in pounds)
Multiply your height by 12.7 (in inches)	Multiply your height by 4.7 (in inches)
Add together your height, weight and base figures.	Add together your height, weight and base figures.
Multiply your age by 6.8	Multiply your age by 4.7
Subtract your age figure from the figure above.	Subtract your age figure from the figure above.

The total is your metabolic rate.

This example is for a man aged 30, who weighs 182 lbs and is 72 inches tall:

Base	= 66
182 lbs x 6.3	= 1147
72 inches x 12.7	= 914
66 + 1147 + 914	= 2127
30 years x 6.8	= 204
2127 - 204	= 1923
Metabolic rate is	1923

This is the amount of calories that the man's body uses at rest. An average, moderately active person will burn about 30% more calories than their metabolic rate.

30% of 1923	= 577
1923 + 577	= 2500

This means, to maintain his current weight, this man needs to consume 2500 calories per day.

But in order to lose weight, he must consume no more than 1923.

This is not 100% accurate but it is a reasonable way of calculating your individual needs, much better than working from one of the approximate tables. The closer you are to the correct amount of calories you require the better. This is because excess calories are converted into body fat.

3500 calories = 1 lb of body fat. This does not sound much, but if for example, you take in excess of 100 calories per day, you will gain approximately 1 lb in weight per month. That's 12 lbs a year and 4 stones over a 5 year period.

Height and Weight Tables

Height and weight tables are regarded as a reliable way of predicting how much you should weigh, depending on your height. In recent years these tables have come under a great deal of criticism.

They were first developed for insurance companies to use as a guideline for making decisions about health risks and mortality. They are based on thousands of people who bought insurance policies, and they show the weight at which the fewest number of policy holders died, this is, the weight that statistically they were most likely to live to.

The actual figures were based on the number of policies, not the number of people. That meant that if a man died who had taken out five polices, his figures would have been counted five times.

Another crucial point is that these tables do not distinguish body weight from body fat. A man that has been body-building for a few years will be, according to these tables, overweight because of his increase in muscle. And someone who is classed as the correct weight by the tables may have a lot of body fat, but not as much muscle.

If you are honest with yourself, you will know if you have got excess body fat or not. If you have, you are overweight.

Diets that Guarantee Weight Loss in Days!

I am sure by now, you have tried every diet you could get your hands on, everything from junk food to fruit juice diets. And I am sure you have heard and tried a lot more weird and wonderful ones than probably I have.

Just think back for a moment, why did you stop all of those diets you have tried in the past, does it go something like this? You start off with good intentions, this is the one that is going to work, you are going to stick to this one no matter what. You stick to the diet for two whole weeks, but you start getting miserable. You have lost some weight, you know that, after all you have been on those bathroom scales everyday for a fortnight, and scales don't lie, do they?

A member of your family comes up to you, one of the children for instance, 'Can I have' and before you realise, you are screaming and shouting at them for no good reason at all. And then there is your partner, have you really been as nice to them as normal? Probably not. Things don't look too good, but you have a bright idea, a way of cheering yourself up. You go to the fridge, open the door and there it is, just sitting there waiting for someone to gently unwrap it. You are tempted, you can imagine the taste of it, you remember the feeling of contentment that you get sitting in the arm chair, bloated with an over-loaded stomach. Oh, happy, happy memories.

No, you must be strong, you slam the fridge door, but it's not over, it is still in there, waiting. You walk away, determined to think about something else completely. But it's no good, you cannot get that scrumptious, calorie filled lovely out of your mind. The temptation is too much for you, so you return to the fridge, open the door, and *scream*! Those lovely little children of yours have eaten *your* only chance of keeping sane. You panic, you look at your watch and your local shop is still open for another fifteen minutes. Great!

You hustle the children next door and run the hundred yards to the shop. Once inside, you look around the shelves, and there they are, calories by the thousand, all looking down at you begging you to buy them. Five minutes later, you enter your front door with a bag of goodies stuffed under your arm.

This is the end of the story, because I am sure you all know how it finishes. You guessed it, you sit down and pig out, binge or what ever else you want to call it. Well that's it, you have broken your diet, you might as well go back to the way you were, at least then you were happy. Weren't you?

Joking aside, this is the case with a lot of people when they try these so called diets. Then of course there are those of you that do have the will power, you will not be beaten, once you start a diet, you stick to it. The first two weeks, great, you have lost weight. Those good old reliable bathroom scales have been working overtime again.

You are amazed, you have lost so much weight, you could kiss your Aunt Bessy's, next door neighbours, sister's friend's uncle, once removed, for giving you this wonderful, life changing diet, or so you think! Great, within a matter of weeks you are down to your target weight. That wasn't too hard now, was it? You relax your eating habits, only slightly, but 'Oh no' you start piling on those lost pounds again. Another depressed dieter.

Why does this happen with every diet I try?

It is actually very straight forward, and I will try to explain it to you as simply as I can.

Most diets are very low in calories, and as we have already established, people can, and do, lose weight very early on. The problem is, it does not continue and most people tend to regain this weight very quickly. What people do not realise is, two thirds of this weight loss is in fact water, something that all these so called experts, who are selling you their diets and pills etc., do know. They also know a lot more, but you can bet your life they ain't going to tell you anything, but I am.

Most low calorie diets are also low in carbohydrates. Both your red blood cells and your brain need blood sugar to enable them to function properly. Blood sugar comes from carbohydrates.

If your body is not getting enough carbohydrates from your diet, your liver starts to break down its own stored sugar and then, sends it into your bloodstream. Once all your liver's stored sugar has been used, the liver starts working on the amino acids from your body's muscle protein, by turning them into sugar. The liver's stored sugar and the muscle proteins are little molecules surrounded by water. Each molecule contains 3 times as much water as stored sugar or protein. This means that every time the liver breaks down an ounce of protein, or stored sugar, 3 ounces of water is released from that cell at the same time. This is then transported to the kidneys and removed from the body as urine.

Now you can understand why you can lose so much weight in the early stages of a diet. You are no thinner however long you spend looking at yourself in the mirror, you have not lost fat, you have just lost water. It is simply a short term side effect caused by not eating enough carbohydrates.

Not only does losing water produce no real benefit, it can also be harmful. Along with water, you are losing essential nutrients and phosphorus that your body needs.

Now you know the reason why you keep seeing these extraordinary advertisements, that absolutely guarantee weight loss in a matter of just a few days. Is it fat you are losing, or is it merely water? I am sure you have tried enough products in the past to decide for yourself.

Desperate Times

Unfortunately, some people get so depressed about the state of their bodies and become so desperate to lose weight that they will try almost anything in order to achieve the results that they are looking for.

Wonder Pills and Fad Diets

We have briefly covered this subject already, but the truth is that there is an enormous amount of money to be made out of such products, the manufacturers know that you are desperate, and this puts them in a very strong position. Any diet that restricts you to a small choice of foods, or does not help you to reduce your calorie intake and increase your calorie expenditure is probably not worth bothering with. A lot of the pills and potions that are available, are nothing more than laxatives.

The Very Low Calorie Diet

Again we have already discussed why these are of no real benefit.

Appetite Suppressants

Many drugs have been available to dieters over the years in order to suppress their cravings for food. These have been shown to have a number of side effects, and once you stop taking them, your appetite does return.

Smoking

Anyone who thinks that smoking will help them lose weight are completely mad, unless of course you are planning on contracting lung cancer. A bit drastic don't you think?

The Body Wrap

There are several different methods available, but they all promise you the same. You will lose inches off your waist, hips and thighs etc., in a matter of minutes.

What happens is, you are weighed and measured and then your entire body is wrapped in wet bandages and then you are left to dry. Once you are dry, the bandages are removed and you are immediately weighed and measured again. Amazingly you weigh lighter and measure smaller. Great, but what's the catch? The catch is that you have lost a lot of water, and as soon as you replace that by having a drink, you will go straight back to how you were before. These wraps are not cheap and in my opinion they are a complete waste of money. The only reason I can possibly think that you might want to have a body wrap, is if it is a special occasion and you want to fit into a particular outfit. If this is the case, fine. But be warned, don't drink too much, you might start popping buttons.

Laxatives

By taking laxatives for long periods of time, you mess around with your body chemistry. Weight loss using laxatives is a very temporary measure and they can become very addictive. Do not get involved with laxatives, the side effects are just not worth it.

The Alternative

The only safe and reliable way to lose weight, is naturally. It took a long time for you to put this weight on, you cannot expect to lose it all in just a few weeks. A natural diet gives you a reasonable length of time in which to lose weight, as well as helps you to develop new eating habits and new attitudes towards food.

A Better Lifestyle – A Better You

By now, you should have a rough idea about the amount of calories you need to consume on a daily basis. You do not have to go on a 'diet' to lose weight, you just need to burn off more calories than you take in. And once you have achieved your ideal weight, you just need to consume the correct amount of calories that your body requires.

It is your lifestyle that you need to change, not just your diet, you need to encourage both your mind and body to eat fewer, and healthier calories. You need to make a commitment to change your life, I can tell you how, but that is it, I cannot do it for you. It is not going to be easy, but it is not going to be as hard as you imagine, I promise.

Fat

It is true that everybody does need a certain amount of fat in their diet. But how much do we really need? I am sure that you will be surprised to know that the amount of fat your body needs per day, is the same amount of fat that you would find in a bowl of oatmeal.

Unfortunately the reality is very different. In a diet based on non natural foods, the average intake of calories is made up by 40% fat. Obtaining this amount of calories from fat, is unhealthy, unwise and definitely unnecessary.

If the calories derived from fat are not converted to energy, they will be stored as body fat and you will put on weight. The average person could do with cutting down their fat intake, by half.

This does not mean that you cannot eat any more of your favourite foods, it just means that you need to set a limit on how much and how often you eat them.

Carbohydrates

Your body can burn off, or use more calories derived from carbohydrates, than calories derived from fats or proteins, therefore, consuming most of your calories from carbohydrates (65 - 75%) is a sensible measure. The problem that confuses many people is that there are two different types of carbohydrates, simple and complex carbohydrates.

Simple carbohydrates supply instant energy to your body and nothing more. They are usually very high in calories and any surplus are stored as fat. This type of carbohydrate is found in chocolate, pastries and sugary snacks.

Complex carbohydrates do contain simple carbohydrates, but they also contain a large amount of starch and fibre. Your body takes longer to break down starch than it does to break down simple carbohydrates. As the starch is broken down, energy is supplied to your body, but this energy is produced in smaller quantities over a longer period of time. This means your stomach feels fuller for longer.

Fibre moves through your digestive system, and as it does, it helps move fats, vitamins and minerals. It also absorbs a lot of water, helping to make your bowel movements much easier. Complex carbohydrates are found in potatoes, whole wheat pasta, spaghetti etc. In the past it was considered that carbohydrates were actually fattening. Do not listen to anyone who says that fibre and complex carbohydrates are not good for you, it is just not true.

Protein

Protein is vital for the growth of skin, nails and hair, it is also vital for the repair and maintenance of the body.   Protein is present in every living thing, so do not be fooled into thinking that you can only get protein from meats, fish and dairy products.   What about the Great British baked bean, it is full of protein.   So are potatoes, soya milk, lentils and grains.

Protein is vital, but excess protein is stored as fat.   There is no reason for consuming large amounts of protein in your daily diet. Exceptions to this may include pregnant or nursing women and people who are badly injured (broken bones or torn muscles).   If you are unsure, consult your doctor.

Foods

Whole wheat bread
Whole grain rice
Whole wheat pasta
Potatoes
Root vegetables
Leaf vegetables
Fresh fruit
Sun dried fruit
Millet
Barley
Oats
Rye
Nuts (not salted peanuts)
Beans
Lentils

These are all low fat and high complex carbohydrate foods.

Red meats
Chocolate
Biscuits
Pastries
Butter
Margarine
Cheese
Full milk
Cream
Crisps
Fried food
Fizzy drinks
Alcohol

These are all high fat foods.

Fresh fruits
Vegetables
Salads
Fish (steamed)
Skimmed milk
Potatoes
White meats
Porridge
Baked beans
Spaghetti
Pasta
Unsweetened fruit juices.

These are all lower fat foods.

I know what you are thinking, you know which foods you should and should not be eating, and you do not want to listen to a lecture about them. But there is more to changing your lifestyle than just the food itself. We have already established that potatoes are low in fat and high in complex carbohydrates. An ideal food you might think, and you would be right, if it is cooked correctly. Boiled and jacket potatoes are excellent, but roast or fried potatoes are swimming in fat.

Oh my goodness, no more chips!

This is the major factor that puts people off eating sensibly, they think that they can no longer eat their favourite foods. Well you can, if you are imaginative and you eat in moderation. Ever heard of the fat-free chip? Well you have now.

Peel a potato and cut into chips.
Place the chips onto a baking try and put to one side.
Set the oven to a moderate heat.
Take an egg, and separate the white.
Throw the yoke away (it is full of fat and cholesterol).
Using a pastry brush, paste the chips with the egg white.
Place the chips into the oven until golden brown.
The chips can be turned over halfway through, and egg white reapplied.

And there you have it, the fat-free chip. It's simple, all you have to do is use your imagination. Don't fry food, grill or steam instead, it is much lower in fat and it tastes just as good.

You need to cut down on meat and animal products. Most meats and animal products, such as milk and cheese are high in fat. Most people do not like the idea of cutting meat out of their diet altogether, but cutting your intake down is sensible. If you insist on eating meat, choose white meat. The redder the meat, the more saturated in fat it is. Chicken, turkey and veal are far less fatty, than lamb, beef and pork. As for milk and cheese, choose skimmed, or at least semi-skimmed milk and change to low fat cheese and yoghurt.

Fish is commonly regarded as a health food, but you need to select it carefully. We often forget about the pollution that is dumped into our seas, untreated sewage etc. Fish frequently show signs of disease, parasites and intestinal worms. And on the increase, both salt and fresh water fish, have been found to be in a cancerous state. Fish oil has been shown to lower cholesterol in the blood, however these oils can be obtained from plant sources.

In general choose carefully, and cook just as carefully.

Try to eat more natural foods, these include:

Vegetables
Grains
Fruit
Nuts
Seeds
Pulses
Yeast
Soya products

Your local supermarket will stock at least 50-60 different food items. Do not be put off or afraid of changing the way you eat. Try it, you might even find that you prefer the new foods to the ones you are used to. Make a commitment, and try something different.

Below is a list of foods and their relevant amount of calories:

	Kcal/25g (1 oz)		Kcal/25g (1 oz)
All-Bran	88	Bacon – raw	135
Weetabix	100	Bacon – grilled	60
Cornflakes	103	Beef – roasted	80
Muesli	100	Beef – corned	84
Bran	51	Chicken – roasted	52
Bread – brown	66	Duck – roasted	89
Bread – white	72	Gammon steak –	
Bread –		grilled	40
wholemeal	68	Ham – boiled	60
Biscuit –		Lamb – roasted	90
chocolate	142		
Biscuit – plain	122	Luncheon meat	92
Biscuit – sweet	141	Pork – roasted	90
Flour – white	99	Sausage – pork	105
Flour –		Veal – roasted	66
wholemeal	68	Turkey – roasted	56
Rice – raw	102	Nut – walnut	151

Rice – boiled	35	Nuts – roasted	
Egg (1) -		peanut	166
standard	80	Honey	82
Egg (1) - white	15	Jam	74
Egg (1) - yolk	65	Peanut butter	170
Butter	211	Sugar	112
Lard	253	Golden syrup	84
Margarine	218	Baked beans	26
Vegetable oil	255	Broad beans	19
White fish – raw	23	Soya beans	29
Fish fingers –		Cabbage	2
raw	54	Leeks	9
Kipper – raw	62	Carrots	7
Salmon – tinned	38	Potatoes – boiled	23
Sardines in oil	81	Potatoes – fried	67
Apples	13	Potatoes – roasted	35
Bananas	22	Mushrooms	2
Dates	70	Swede	7
Grapes	15	Cucumbers	3
Lemons	2	Beer and stout	10
Oranges	10	Gin	65
Rhubarb	2	Brandy	65
Raisins – dried	70	Rum	65
Sultanas – dried	71	Whisky	65
Cheese – cheddar	117	Wine	18
Cheese – cottage	31	Sherry	33
Cream – double	104	Cordial – undiluted	30
Cream – single	40	Orange juice	16
Milk – whole	18	Tomato juice	5
Milk – skimmed	9	Tonic water	10
Yoghurt – fat-			
free	12		
Yoghurt – fruit	22		

Remember you still need to obtain most of your calories from complex carbohydrates.

Today, good nutrition is considered a lot more important than it used to be. With this in mind, most food manufacturers, do display the nutritional values on their food products. A typical example is:

Nutritional Information

Typical values	Amount per 100g	Amount per serving(202g)
Energy	201 kJ/48 kcal	405 kJ/96 kcal
Protein	2.0g	4.0g
Carbohydrates (of which are sugars)	7.2g (0.8g)	14.6g (1.7g)
Fat (of which are saturates)	1.2g (0.2g)	2.4g (0.4g)
Fibre	0.5g	1.1g
Sodium	0.4g	0.7g

A lot of people look at these tables and get utterly confused. What you are looking for, is simply the amount of calories (shown as kcal) and how the calories are made up, proteins, fats and carbohydrates. Forget about the kilojoules, these are just the metric version of the kilocalories.

The information given, is given in two different amounts, but this is not necessarily the amount for the overall product. Confused?

If the information shown is for a tinned product, for example, the amounts shown are for 100 grams and 202 grams. But you must be aware that some manufactures do not show the figures for the overall product. The overall weight of the food could be 500 grams, so if you were planning to eat the whole tin of food, you would have to multiply the figures for 100 grams by 5 in order to find the correct amount of calories.

Also, remember that you are looking for a high level of complex carbohydrates, a moderate level of protein and a low level of fat. Obviously it is difficult to spend time, looking at which food contains which amount of calories when you are at your local super market. I have listed a small amount of foods already, but suggest that you invest in a calorie counting book (available from all good bookshops). This will list most foods and their calorie make up, so you will know what foods to look for, before you actually go shopping.

A good tip is, make a shopping list before you go and stick to it, do not go wandering off down the aisles looking at what goodies you can spend your money on.

Food for Thought and the Fat-Busters

Are you tired, depressed, upset or anxious? If the answer is yes to any one of these questions, it could be down to the foods you do or do not eat. In certain cases, certain foods upset the balance of our bodies. Scientists are now beginning to look into how foods, or the ingredients they contain, can be used to alter states of consciousness, improve moods and help relaxation.

What is clear, is, certain foods taken in large amounts or in combination with other foods, may alter the way you feel. Knowing which foods do what, can be useful when planning meals, e.g., you do not want to be eating foods that are full of stimulants late at night.

There are over 200 different herbs and foods that are known to have an effect on us, in one way or another. Here are just a few.

Bananas: Contain tryptophan, an amino acid which can induce
               sleep. It also has anti-depressant properties.

Yams: Contain a phytohormone which is very similar to the
               female sex hormone, oestrogen. It is believed that
               women who are nearing the menopause, or who have
               had a hysterectomy could get a benefit from
               regularly eating yams.

Mangos: Contain substances which may have anti-depressant
               properties.

Horseradish: Contains a mild stimulant.

Parsley: Contains a mild stimulant.

Pepper: Can be used as a stimulant.

Nutmeg: Can cause hallucinations.

Watermelon: Contains a natural diuretic, which can help remove excess fluid.

White cabbage: In some countries this is used to treat stomach ulcers.

Chicken soup: Contain the same chemicals that are found in modern day cold remedies.

Garlic: Is said to increase resistance from infection. (colds etc.)

Onion: Contains a substance which has a clot preventive effect.

Carrot: Contains a substance in the seeds which appears to have aphrodisiac properties for women.

Wine: Small consumption, can help protect against heart disease.

This section will be of most interest to you. These are the foods that incorporated in your diet can either help or hinder you.

Broccoli: Contains a mild thyroid suppressing substance.

Swede: Contains a thyroid suppressing substance.

Soya Bean: Contains a thyroid suppressing substance.

Peas: Contains a thyroid suppressing substance.

Cabbage: Contains a mild thyroid suppressing substance.

What is the thyroid and what does it do?

The thyroid gland is very important, it is situated just below the Adam's apple and regulates the metabolism. It is common for overweight and people over 35 to have a thyroid gland that is not as effective as it should be. Therefore, if you do have a thyroid problem, avoiding the above foods may be a sensible measure.

Beetroot: Believe it or not, beetroot can help you lose weight. It contains alkaloid betaine, which has a significant benefit on the liver by detoxifying it and stimulating its normal function. If the liver is not functioning normally, it cannot break down fat, and transport it through the body as effectively as it should. Raw beetroot juice, taken on a regular basis is said to help fat mobilisation as well as toning the whole body. A natural colorant in beetroot has been shown to have both anti-cancer and anti-ageing properties.

Seaweed: It is useful for nerves, constipation, arthritis and maintaining good skin and nails. But most of all, it is known for its strong effect on the metabolism, helping to mobilise fat and correct an under active thyroid. Kelp tablets can often be of use in losing weight, and can be easily obtained from health shops.

Celery: The stem, leaves and seeds all contain a chemical which is used by herbalists to help and prevent colds. It is also known to help with arthritis, calming the nerves and to help banish cellulite. Celery must be eaten raw, once it has been heated it loses all of its health-giving properties.

Raw food: Eating raw fruit and vegetables can help with weight loss because, you feel that you have eaten more than you really have, due to the fact that they take a lot more chewing and swallowing, and therefore take longer to eat. Also, because this type of food is full of raw fibre, it gives your stomach the bulk it associates with being full. The thought of eating raw food, especially raw vegetables can be off putting, but do try it. I will admit that it is not my favourite food, but you do get used to it. When eating raw food, drinking plenty of fresh water does help to wash it down.

I Will Lose Weight by Not Eating!

Absolute rubbish.

It is a preconceived idea that not eating is the best way to lose weight. If this is what you believe, I am sorry, but you are wrong. It is all to do with your metabolic rate.

Your metabolic rate is the rate at which your body burns off calories when it is at rest. Over the years, our bodies have learned to control their own metabolic rate, in order to prevent starvation. Simply put, if you stop eating, your metabolic rate slows down, which limits the amount of calories your body uses to function. It is your body's way of surviving without food.

What does this all mean? It means, if you decide to stop eating in order to lose weight, your body will take longer to burn off your body fat, than it would if you were eating. Defeats the object really, doesn't it?

Will Eating Just One Meal a Day Help Me Lose Weight?

No. The actual act of eating increases your metabolic rate, which in turn burns off more calories. Therefore it is important, if you want to lose weight, to eat regularly, every day.

When to Eat, That's the Question

We have covered what to eat and how often to eat, but we have not covered when to eat. Believe it or not, this is just as important. Today's hustle and bustle lifestyle means that we tend to eat convenient, unhealthy snacks, or even miss out meals altogether in favour of keeping that business meeting, or getting the shopping done before it is time to pick up the children. Of course you have daily commitments to keep, we all do, life does not revolve around the dinner table. But we are getting into an increasingly bad habit of eating little during the day, and then making up for it in the evening.

Time and time again I hear people complaining because they only eat one, healthy meal a day, and still have trouble controlling their weight. We know how important it is to eat on a regular basis, in order to increase our metabolic rate, and therefore allow our bodies to burn off more calories at rest.

Let's take an example:

You get up at say 7.00 a.m., you go to work, and basically eat very little. You get home around 6.00 p.m. and eat your main meal about 7.00 p.m.. Your metabolic rate has been on a go slow from that morning (at least 12 hours). You eat your main meal, and slowly your metabolic rate starts to speed up. Great, your body is using up more calories at rest. But, in order to control, or lose weight, you need to be burning off either the same amount of calories, or more calories than your body requires.

It does not matter if you are eating one, or three meals a day, if you eat your main meal in the evening, say about 7.00 p.m., the chances are that you will do very little afterwards, am I right?

Odds on, you have had a hard day at the office, or with the children, you have had your dinner and now it's time to relax. All you want to do is sit down in front of the television until it is time for bed. Nothing wrong with that, I like nothing better in an evening, than getting comfortable in front of the television and watching a few soaps. But what is your body doing?

Yes, yes, it's burning off calories, we know all that, but is it burning off the required amount of calories in order for you to lose or control your weight?

The answer is no. Most of us eat far too late in the day. If you go to a restaurant, what time do you go, 7.30 p.m. - 8.30 p.m.? By the time you have finished eating, it can quite easily be 9.00 p.m. - 10 p.m. Then as soon as you get home, or shortly after, you end up going to bed.

The great disadvantage of eating late at night is, that you are reducing the amount of available time that you may have to increase your metabolic rate and so, burn off more calories.

Here is a list of activities, which show the approximate calories, per minute that are required.

(L) Refers to light

(M) Refers to moderate

(S) Refers to strenuous

Activity	Calories Used Per Minute
Standing	1.7
Sitting	1.4
Walking (slow pace)	2.5
Walking (normal pace)	3.5
Walking (fast pace)	6.5
Walking (uphill, with load)	7.5
Sleeping	1.0
Cooking	1.8
Washing + Ironing	3.5
Cleaning (L)	3.0
Gardening (L)	3.5
Gardening (M)	4.5
Gardening (S)	6.0
Playing Golf	3.5
Playing Tennis	6.5
Playing Squash	8.0
Playing Football	7.5
Swimming (L)	6.5
Swimming (S)	8.5

As you can see, sitting watching the television, or being tucked up in bed, uses up the least amount of calories possible. Now you can see why it makes sense to consume most of your calories, early on in the day, allowing your body time to naturally burn off any excess calories. If you are resourceful, you will be surprised how easily you can change the way you eat.

Always eat a good breakfast. Not only does this help fuel your body for the day ahead, (as long as it contains plenty of complex carbohydrates) it also ensures that your metabolic rate gets off to a good start. If it is at all possible, eat your main meal at mid day, and then eat just a light snack later on in the day. Try not to eat anything, especially high calorie food after about 7.00 p.m.. If you are one of those people who have a tendency to nibble in front of the television, *don't*!

It is totally unnecessary, and is usually done simply out of boredom. Find something else to do with your hands, (no smoking) take up knitting, or give a friend a massage, anything just to keep yourself occupied. I know it is easier said than done, but it can be done. If the temptation is too great, chomp on a carrot or a stick of celery. The alternative of course, is chewing some chewing gum.

I realise lads, that you have no intention whatsoever of giving up your can of beer, while you are watching the football on the television. This is of course up to you, but you can cut your amount down, and change your food intake accordingly. Remember a pint of beer contains 160 calories, this means that you need to walk for about an hour for every pint you consume in order to burn off these calories.

Alcohol

This is not going to be a lecture but, I am going to point out that alcohol is, in itself, the cause of a great number of overweight cases. Apart from that, I am sure you are all aware of the health factors with consuming too much alcohol. Slow down, make your drink last longer, as well as cut down.

Alcohol is something that is rammed down our throats from a very early age. Look at all the millions of pounds spent a year advertising on the television and in the major newspapers. These advertising campaigns are predominately targeted at the young. This type of mass advertising can quite easily lead to long-term addiction, and I am not just talking about alcoholics.

The peer pressure that is placed on the young to drink is huge, especially with teenagers. It is considered cool to drink and to be seen drinking in the right pub or night-club. The problem arises years down the road, when the once teenagers become adults, and have to deal with adult stresses and responsibilities. When they want to relax or get away from a particular problem, what do they do, where do they go? They go off to the pub or open a few cans in front of the television, the same thing that they have been doing for years, it has become a habit.

Later on, it can lead to addiction. When they are having trouble with work or with a relationship, too many people time and time again automatically turn to alcohol to solve or to help forget about their problems. Of course it solves nothing, and sooner or later they do start to remember, and maybe one of the problems they were trying to forget about was, a weight problem.

Before I finish my little sermon, for those of you who say that you need to drink in order to enjoy yourself, if this is true, you must lead a sad and very boring life.

All I am saying is slow down and cut down, and if life really is that boring, and you cannot think of any other way to get some pleasure out of life, you can always revert to sex. It is better for you, it is definitely cheaper and you might even burn off a few extra calories while you are at it. (A lot more than you would do if you were stood at the bar supping all night.)

A Bit of What You Fancy Does You Good!

A truer word has never been be spoken.

OK folks this is what you have all been waiting for. How many times have you wanted to eat that fresh cream cake, or that piece of chocolate, but resisted the urge? If you cut out all the sweet and nice things that you enjoy eating, all at once, two things will happen. Firstly for most people, you will become very depressed and very cranky, very quickly. This is because your body is having withdrawal symptoms. It has been used to having all the high calorie types of food that you have been feeding it. The second thing is, the cravings.

I am sure that you all know what I am talking about. You can go for so long, but after a while the cravings get too great to ignore. Cravings usually lead towards bingeing, and once you start bingeing, you have got problems. If anybody knows anything about bingeing, I do.

Quite a few years ago, I decided to cut out chocolate altogether, something that I adore (some of you may be able to relate to this). For the first few weeks I did not even think about chocolate, but this did not last for long.

It must of been about four or five weeks down the line, and I was shopping in my local supermarket. I went down the aisle, and there it was, my favourite chocolate, bars and bars of it. I quickly did a U-turn, but it was no good, I started to get that feeling of need inside of me, I had seen it and I wanted it. I went back to the chocolate and picked up two bars and put them in my trolley. I will put them in the fridge when I get home and leave them there just to prove I can have them in the house without actually eating them. Ha, who was I trying to kid?

As soon as I arrived home, in the fridge they went, I slammed the door and forgot about them, until about 9 o'clock that evening. It was just too much for me, I knew they were there and I knew that the only way to satisfy my need, was to eat just a small amount of that chocolate. I fetched a bar from the fridge, took it up stairs to the bedroom, switched the television on, and sat down to enjoy myself. I ripped open the wrapper, broke off a square, and popped it into my mouth. Ecstasy, the pleasure I got was incredible, I had gone far too long without this simple form of satisfaction, I wanted to hold onto this feeling of contentment for as long as humanly possible. Needless to say, I ended up eating both bars of chocolate in a very short space of time. Surprised? Probably not, perhaps you have done the same thing. The fact is, a lot of people do have the same sort of problem. Oh, one thing I forgot to mention, the two bars of chocolate that I ate were 400 grams each, that's 32 ounces of chocolate eaten in less than two hours. That little lot added up to 5280 calories, and then guess what I did? That's right, I went to bed. What I should of done was to go for a 25 mile walk, that would have burnt it off, just.

The magic word here is moderation. Don't go mad like I did, it just throws a spanner in the works and confuses your body. Eat the nice things in life with pleasure, but ration them, treat yourself say two or three times a week. And don't think, great it's a treat day I am going to pig out at McDonald's and then eat chocolate for the rest of the day, because it is not on. Even on treat days watch and count your calories. Remember you are retraining your appetite, treat but do not binge. A good tip is, try never to keep too much nice food in the house at one time. If it is there in front of you, the temptation to eat it is far greater than it would be if you had to go out and buy it.

Exercise

From the beginning of time, up to just a few centuries ago, people had to be fit in order to survive. Every day demanded long, hard physical work, whether it was hunting for food, or spending 16 hours a day on the land, people worked hard, that's the way it was, people did not know any different, it was accepted, and it was the norm.

Today, the norm is getting from A to B, however short the distance, by use of modern technology. Today's society has learned to rely more on technology than they do on themselves. When was the last time you went outside humping buckets of water around, or spent a couple of hours chopping wood, so you could keep both you and your family warm?

Life today is all about taking the easy option, and most of us do. We don't even have to get up out of our chairs to change the channel on our televisions any more.

What about the future, are we going to be able to live a full and productive life without even having to leave the comfort of our own homes?

The fact is, we are living in a modern world, but our body make up, is still basically that of the Stone Age.

There is a vast amount of evidence that shows that, without regular physical work or exercise, we are leaving our bodies wide open to a whole range of mental and physical ailments.

Regular exercise has been proven to reduce the risks of heart related diseases, reduce blood pressure, cholesterol levels in the blood, and to help people cope better with both stress and depression.

Physical activity exercises the heart, which increases the efficiency of the lungs. This means that every time your heart beats and every time you breathe, more oxygen which is carried by more blood is pumped around your body. This helps to reduce your heart beat at rest, and also helps your heart cope a lot better with the extra demands that may be put upon it.

Exercise encourages the release of endorphins, which are hormones in the brain. The release of these, creates a feeling of happiness and well-being. Some people class these as the body's natural drug, enabling you to feel a natural high. This is why depressed people who exercise, recover a lot quicker than those who don't.

Having to cope with stress seems to be on the increase, whether it's work related, financial or any one of the other growing reasons.

We all need a certain amount of stress in our lives, but today's world of high mortgage rates and lack of job security, forces us to take on more stresses than are good for us. Large companies, concerned with health factors, and with the amount of lost working days due to stress related illness, are now sending their employees on stress management courses, in order to cut these figures down. It has been proven that exercise can help reduce stress levels and help people relax and cope better with day to day problems. Do not, in any way underestimate stress, believe me, it's a killer.

A lot of people think that exercise will encourage them to eat even more. This is a preconceived idea, and in fact the reverse is true, exercise will actually suppress your craving for food.

Studies have shown that, the only way to lose weight and maintain that loss over a long period of time is to incorporate exercise into your daily routine.

If you are not prepared to exercise, then I am sorry, but you have wasted your money on this book. Exercise is the fundamental key to weight loss and weight control. You cannot do one successfully without the other.

If you think that you can lose and control your weight just by what you eat, forget it, you are wasting your time. Stop reading this right now, throw it in the bin, get a bar of your favourite chocolate and sit yourself down in front of the television.

Still with us? Great. You have just proved to yourself that you are serious about losing weight.

The benefits of exercise are countless both mentally and physically. The fitter you become, the more confident you feel about yourself, the better you feel and the better you look. It is, as simple as that. This is why exercise is not only crucial for overcoming a weight problem, but is crucial for a better, healthier and happier life.

It is important that if you are over 35 and/or overweight that you are thoroughly checked out by your doctor before you start any form of exercise.

Your heart is a muscle, and unless it is exercised correctly, it will grow weak. After 24 hours of inactivity muscle tissue will begin to deteriorate and only regular exercise can prevent this from happening. Before you start to exercise, it is a good idea to find out just how fit you are at present, and, the safe limits in which you should exercise. You can do this by taking your pulse. When you feel your pulse, what you are actually feeling is the flow of blood pressing against, and expanding the walls of your arteries as it is being pumped around the body. You can take your pulse at several different points around the body, but the two most common places are, the wrist and the neck.

When you are taking your pulse at the wrist, turn your hand, palm side up. Place two fingers from the other hand, gently at the base of the thumb and wrist joint. If you prefer to take your pulse at your neck, again place two fingers at the side of the neck, just below the jaw. Once you have decided which point you prefer, place the two fingers on that point and move them slightly, until you can feel a strong pulse. Never use your thumb as this has its own pulse and may cause confusion. Take your pulse sitting down, first thing in the morning. This is when your pulse will be at its lowest. Count how many times your pulse beats in 15 seconds and multiply this by 4. This figure will be your base rate. During exercise, your pulse will increase rapidly, but there is a limit which it is not safe to go over. This limit differs from person to person. To find the pulse range in which you will get the most benefit, perform the following:

Take both your age and your base rate and add them together.

Subtract this from 220.

Multiply this figure by 0.6

Add your base rate.

This is your lowest rate.

Take both your age and base rate and add them together.

Subtract from 220.

Multiply this figure by 0.8

Add your base rate.

This is your highest limit.

E.g. If you are 26, and your base rate is 64:

26 + 64	= 90
220 - 90	= 130
130 x 0.6	= 78
78 + 64	= 142
Your lowest rate	= <u>142</u>
26 + 64	= 90
220 - 90	= 130
130 x 0.8	= 104
104 + 64	= 168
Your highest rate	= <u>168</u>

If during exercise your pulse is below your lowest rate, you are not exercising hard enough to get any real benefit. But if it is above your highest level, you are pushing yourself too hard and this could be dangerous.

As soon as you have stopped exercising, take your pulse. It should be between your upper and lower limits. One minute later, take your pulse again. The difference between the two readings, shows the rate at which your heart is recovering. As you get fitter your heart will recover quicker. After about 10 minutes take your pulse again. This time your pulse rate should be below 100 beats a minute. The lower your pulse, the fitter you are.

Each time you exercise take your pulse 3 times as stated and record your results. This will show how you are improving and also help you to keep motivated.

Many of us today think that we do not need to exercise because we do so much during our normal day to day lives. We spend all day looking after the children, cooking and cleaning, or rushing about at work and this is enough exercise for any of us. Exercise and fat loss go together hand in hand, but it can be a little confusing. Just because, at the end of the day you are shattered, does not mean that you have necessarily done the right sort, or the right amount of exercise to burn off the required amount of calories.

E.g. Two women, the same height and weight, both eat the same amount of calories per day, and both work in the same office environment.

Woman A does some form of exercise, 4 times during the day, and this helps her burn off 446 calories more, than Woman B. Work this out over a period of, a year, and that adds up to 162,344 calories.

Of course this is only an example, but you can see what effect just a little amount of exercise can have.

If you exercise for, say 15 minutes a day every day, over a period of time you would get fitter and feel better. You will also increase your metabolic rate, which in turn will help burn off more calories. But, you would not lose any fat whatsoever. Short periods of exercise burn glucose, only long-term exercise, 30 minutes and over, 4-6 times a week will burn fat. The energy that is used for short periods of exercise, even if it is very high intensive, is virtually all derived from stored carbohydrates. Only with moderate to long-term exercise, 30 minutes and over, will your body begin to obtain its energy from stored body fat.

To burn off fat, you need to exercise at least 3 times a week, for 30 minutes to an hour at a time. Better results will be obtained by exercising 4-5 times a week.

Do not try and squash all your exercise time for the week together, 3 hours, twice a week etc. It will not work. The same applies with spreading your exercise time out, 15 minutes, 7 days a week, you will not get the results you are looking for.

Don't say that you are too busy to exercise, you are just making excuses.

Remember: Don't try to find time to exercise, *make* time!

There are two basic types of exercise, isometric and isotonic.

Isometric, is mainly muscle tension exercises such as weightlifting and body-building. If a muscle is put under repeated large amounts of pressure, it will gradually grow.

Isotonic, or aerobic exercise, puts your body under steady amounts of stress which builds strength, stamina and suppleness. Swimming, running and aerobics, are all types of isotonic exercise. The main portion of your exercise routine should be isotonic, but do try and incorporate some muscle tension exercises into your workouts at least once a week.

Woman A	kcal used	Woman B	kcal used
A.M.			
6.30: Get up	30	6.30: Get up.	30
6.45: 45 minute run.	338	6.45: Has a cup of coffee, and watches TV.	63
7.30: Shower, breakfast, gets ready for work.	120	7.30: Shower, breakfast, gets ready for work.	120
8.30: Walks to work (normal speed).	105	8.45: Goes to work by car.	51
9.00: Works in office environment.	420	9.00: Works in office environment.	420
P.M.			
1.00: Walks with colleagues for 30 mins, sits and eats lunch.	147	1.00: Sits down and eats lunch.	84
2.00: Works in office environment.	480	2.00: Works in office environment.	480
5.30: Walks home.	105	5.30: Drives home.	51
6.00: Prepares dinner/house work.	165	6.00: Prepares dinner/house work.	165
7.00: Sits down watching the TV for 3.5 hrs.	480	7.00: Sits down watching the TV for 3.5 hrs.	480
Goes to bed.		Goes to bed.	
	2205		1759

Warming Up

Before you begin any form of exercise, it is important to spend 5-10 minutes warming up. By doing this, you are not only preparing your body for exercise, but you are also reducing the risks of obtaining any injuries.

Warm up by gently stretching all the muscle groups throughout the body.

Arms and Shoulders

Stand with your feet; shoulder width apart. Lift both your arms up in front of you. Pass them as close to your ears as possible, and continue around to form a complete circle. Continue to perform circular motions for 8-10 seconds. Shake your arms out, and repeat again, but this time changing the direction of your arms.

Neck

Stand upright, feet facing forward. Look down, placing your chin onto your chest. From this position, slowly move your head in a clockwise circular motion. Continue for 8-10 seconds. Repeat, but this time in an anti-clockwise circular motion.

Torso

Face forward, feet; shoulder width apart. Place your hands on your hips and twist your upper body to the left, hold for a second, then return to the starting position. Perform this 8-10 times and then stop. Repeat, but this time twisting your body to the right.

Stand, feet; shoulder width apart. Place your right hand onto the side of your right thigh, and your left hand on the side of your left thigh. Bend your body to the right, so that your right hand moves towards your right knee, return to the starting position. Perform this 8-10 times. Repeat this movement but this time bending your body to the left.

Calves and Hamstrings

Stand, feet; shoulder width apart. Clasp your hands together behind your back. Keep your knees locked, and bend forward until you feel the muscles in the back of your legs beginning to pull. Gently rock up and down so you can feel your muscles tighten and relax. Repeat 8-10 times.

Stand with all your weight on your right leg. Curl your left leg slowly beneath you and hold it for a count of three. (The bottom section of your leg should be held horizontal to the floor.) Straighten your leg and lock out your knee. Perform this 8- 10 times. Repeat the exercise but this time curling your right leg.

Thighs

Stand next to a wall or a high-backed chair for support. Stand, feet shoulder width apart with one hand on the wall/chair. Bend your knees as though you were about to sit down. Keep your back straight and bend until you can feel the muscles in your thighs starting to pull. Hold that position for a second, then return to the starting position. (At this point, do not lock out your knees. This will ensure that constant pressure is placed on your thighs throughout the whole exercise.) Perform this 8-10 times, then and only then lock out your knees.

Abdomen

Lie on your back, knees bent and feet flat on the floor. Place your hands on your thighs, and your chin onto your chest. Move your hands slowly towards your knees by lifting your torso 6-8 inches off the floor. Return to the starting position and repeat 10-20 times. Do not rest in between repetitions, as this takes the constant pressure off your abdominals.

Your whole body should now be warmed up, and you should be ready to begin your exercise. Whatever form of exercise you choose is entirely up to you, but choose an exercise that you feel comfortable doing. If you are not comfortable, you are more likely to quit after a short period of time. Here are a few ideas that you might like to consider.

Running/Jogging

Running is an ideal way of building both strength and stamina, but I would not recommend this for people who are more than one and a half to two stones overweight. The excess weight will put a lot of stress and pressure onto your joints, especially your knees. The advantage of running is that it costs you absolutely nothing.

But, if you do decide to take up running, it is important to invest in a good pair of running shoes, do not wear cheap alternatives. Running shoes are designed for running, they have cushioned soles, which helps to lessen the jarring effect on the joints and they are also much more comfortable. Buy a pair which are a good fit, and take a thick pair of socks with you when you are trying them on. Thick socks should always be worn when running, they help soak up sweat, and prevent blisters. Try to work out your route in advance, and stick to it. Also try to avoid running alongside busy main roads, breathing in exhaust fumes is not really very healthy.

Swimming

Experts believe that swimming is the best all-round exercise. It equally develops strength, stamina and suppleness. It is also ideal if you are overweight because the water actually supports your weight, so you can exercise with no added pressure on your joints.

Aerobics

Aerobics is a great way to firm up your body and develop a strong heart. Aerobics is usually done in large groups which can help with motivation. But if you prefer to do this on your own, you can. Workout videos are easily obtainable. A preconceived idea is that aerobics can only be enjoyed by women. This is not true, so come on men, get your leotards out!

Aqua Aerobics

Aqua aerobics is simply aerobics performed in water. This can be done by people who find normal aerobics too difficult, due to injuries or back problems etc. Just like swimming the water takes the pressure off your joints enabling you to exercise in relative comfort.

Squash

Squash is a very fast, very high intensive sport. It is great fun, but you need to be fairly fit in order to enjoy it to the full. It is not really suitable for someone who is starting to exercise for the first time.

Weight Training

Weight training is brilliant for strengthening and toning the whole body. Many people, especially women think that by using weights they will end up looking like Arnold Schwarzenegger. If you use low weights and do a high amount of repetitions, you will tone up your muscles, not increase their size. On the other hand if you fancy looking like Arnold, use heavier weights and do fewer repetitions.

Before using any weights, learn how to use them correctly. Weights are perfectly safe, if you use them correctly. If in doubt, ask. If you fancy trying weight training, most leisure centres have facilities and have induction courses, showing you how to use them correctly and safely.

Ladies, if you are a little bit shy about pumping iron in front of men, your local leisure centre will more than likely do a number of ladies only sessions. Why not give them a ring and find out.

These are just a few of the many forms of exercise which you can choose from, but if you are not into sport, or you do not fancy the idea of jumping up and down in front of a pack of complete strangers, don't panic.

A lot of people are embarrassed about exercising in front of others, especially those who are overweight. It seems like a vicious circle, you need to exercise because you are overweight, but you refuse to exercise because you are overweight.

There is another way, but before you all get excited thinking that you can lose weight without really having to exercise, don't; exercise is a must.

This form of exercise can be done in private, it can be done whilst listening to music, watching the television, or even while you are looking after the children. You can do it all year round, without even having to take a step outside the front door. You can do this if you are fat, thin, young or old, it does not matter if you are fit, or if you have never done a day's exercise in your life. Anyone and everyone can do this, there are no exceptions.

Welcome to the World of the Rebounder

The rebounder has been around for quite a few years, you will probably find one hidden away in a corner of your local leisure centre gathering dust. They are brilliant, but they don't seem to be very popular, heaven knows why.

A rebounder is basically a little trampoline, set about 6-8 inches off the ground. They come in all different shapes and sizes and can quite easily be stored tidily out of the way until you want to use it. The basic principle is simply to bounce up and down. You can swing your arms, skip, jump, or just bounce in time to some music. It is so simple, and enjoyable, that you will not even consider this to be a form of exercise.

Rebounding is the anti-exerciser's way of exercising. It does what all the other forms of isotonic exercise do; strengthens your heart and lungs, increases levels of stamina and suppleness, tones the muscles throughout the body, and generally does you the world of good. The rebounder can be used if you have had an injury, or even if you are riddled with arthritis. Rebounders are used in rehabilitation, and even people in their seventies and eighties have been reported to have had noticeable benefits from regular use. Even if you have great difficulty in walking, you can still achieve benefits, instead of standing you simply sit down on the rebounder and bounce. Rebounders can be obtained from all good sport shops, and if you think you cannot do this, because you are so overweight you might break it, think again. You can buy heavy duty models! There is no excuse, so why not bounce yourself to a fitter, healthier and slimmer lifestyle.

Cooling Down

Cooling down, once you have finished exercising, is just as important as warming up. When you are exercising, blood rushes to the muscles that are being used. It is then pumped back to the heart and around the rest of the body. If you suddenly stop exercising, the blood can 'pool' in a certain part of the body, instead of returning back to the heart and brain. This can cause a sickness and dizzy feeling.

To cool down, perform the same exercises as you did to warm up.

What to Expect

Once you start to exercise, you will soon be aware of some changes. Some people feel a lack of energy for the first few days, this is because your body is not used to the extra workload. Hold in there, this is only a temporary measure. Most certainly, the morning after you have started your exercise routine, and a few mornings after that, you will be cursing the fact that you ever bought this book. Due to lack of use, your muscles will be tender and a bit uncomfortable. Again, this is only a temporary measure. The turning point for most people is around six weeks. If you can last this long, (you can, and you will) your body will become used to regular exercise, and you will not find exercising such an effort. After six months, you will become hooked, you will find that you actually enjoy exercising and that you don't even want to miss out on one single workout. Believe me, this will happen, so if you are struggling during the early days, just think on, and keep focused.

Points to Remember

Never exercise on a full stomach, leave at least two hours after eating before commencing any form of exercise.

Do not jump straight into a marathon. Everyone, especially those of you who are overweight and/or over 35, should start off slowly and gradually build up both the length of time and the intensity of your workouts. Remember to monitor and record your pulse rate.

If you try something and find that you don't like it, do not give up, just try something different.

And most importantly never ever start exercising tomorrow, because tomorrow never comes.

The Fun Way to Lose Weight

Doctors have now discovered that kissing increases thyroid activity, (which helps burn off more calories) and every time you kiss, you burn off three calories. So, what are you waiting for?

Motivation

We have established along time ago that you do want to lose weight, but the reason that you are most likely to fail in your endeavour will be due to a lack of motivation.

Here are a few tips that I am sure will help you.

If you have always been overweight, try and find a picture of someone who is the ideal weight that you would like to be. Be realistic about this, if you are 20 stone, there is no point in getting hold of a picture of a supermodel, because you are never going to look like that. If the truth be known, you don't want to be. Most of these glamorous supermodels are actually underweight. Be realistic, find a picture of someone about the same age as you, but slimmer. Look through magazines and newspapers, you will be able to find one somewhere.

If you used to be slim, but have managed to pile on some extra pounds over the years, look through your drawers and find an old photograph of yourself when you were slimmer. Once you have got your picture, get someone to take a photograph of you. (if at all possible, in your underwear, but if not, fully clothed will do) This will enable you to see what you actually look like at the present time, mirrors do not give you a true image of yourself. Put the date on the back of the photograph, and place both pictures side by side, somewhere, where you will look at them every day.

This is important as it ensures that you keep your goal clearly in your mind. It is surprising how easy it is to forget your goals and become unfocused.

Every two or three months, have a photograph taken again, and see how you are progressing. If it is at all possible, have the photographs taken in exactly the same position as your original one, same pose, same distance away from the camera, same clothes etc. This way it is easier to notice your improvements. Keep all these pictures together as a record of your success.

If you know someone else who would like to lose weight, a friend or family member, why not consider having them as your motivation partner. Use each other to help push one another through the bad times, especially with exercise. Some people do find exercising alone very dull and boring, and if you decide that you just cannot be bothered with exercise today, your partner can encourage you to get your backside into gear. After all, by saying, 'No, I can't be bothered,' not only are you letting yourself down, but you are also letting your partner down.

Keep a record of your pulse rates, so that you can see how you are progressing and how fit you are becoming.

The Plan

This is crucial. Without a plan you will not know what you are doing, or where you are going. Does a builder build a house without a plan? Is a multi-million pound corporation successful, without some sort of plan? Does a bank robber rob a bank without a plan? Of course not.

Know what you are doing, and when you are doing it. It does not have to be fancy, just write down what you intend to do over the next seven day period.

E.g.:

Monday	Walk to and from work.
Tuesday	Go to the gym after work.
Wednesday	Walk the dog twice as far as normal.
Thursday	Get off the bus two stops earlier when you go shopping.
Friday	Walk the children to school, instead of taking them by car.
Saturday	Go swimming.
Sunday	Take a long walk, after your midday meal.

This is probably ideal for someone who has never exercised before. It is important to start off slowly, and then build up both the amount of time and the intensity of your workouts. Put your plans down on paper, and stick to them. If you do have a motivation partner why not work your plans out together.

Summary

Be aware of the health risks.

Do not talk yourself out of changing your appearance.

Lose weight because *you* want to.

Eat regularly, every day.

Do not consume too many, or too few calories.

Think about what you eat and derive most of your calories from complex carbohydrates.

Cut down on your fat intake.

Cut down on your alcohol intake.

Treat yourself, but do not binge.

Find ways to help keep yourself motivated.

Exercise sensibly as well as regularly

Have a plan.

Be sensible, create a better lifestyle and a better you.

Having read this book, I hope you will look at losing weight in a totally new light, and realise that the best way to lose weight permanently, is naturally. Read and reread the information until you really understand everything you need to know. Once you understand it, stick to it and change your life for the better.

Remember you *can* do it, if *you* want to.

Good luck and God bless.

If you want to, you can.
If you persist, you will.
If you waver, you won't.
If you don't, you never will.